Ultimate
Questions

John Blanchard

W9-CHX-940

EP BOOKS

EP BOOKS Faverdale North, Darlington. DL3 0PH.
England

EP BOOKS P.O. Box 614, Carlisle. PA 17013 USA

©Evangelical Press 1987
This edition 2010

ISBN 978 085234 7225

British Library Cataloguing-in-Publication Data
available

Printed and bound in Great Britain by The Charlesworth
Group, Wakefield. West Yorkshire

Life is full of questions. Some are trivial, some more serious — and some tremendously important.

Even as you read these words you may have questions about your health, your financial situation, your job, your family or your future.

But the greatest, the ultimate questions, are about God and your relationship to him. Nothing in life is more important than this. Good health, financial stability, secure employment, a contented family and a hopeful future are all things that people want. Yet even these are temporary and eventually pointless unless you have a living relationship with God, one that is clear and certain — and will last for ever.

3

In the following pages you will discover why such a relationship is so urgently needed — and how it is possible.

The questions that follow are the most serious and important that anyone could ask. The answers are those that everyone needs. Please read these pages thoroughly and carefully — and if necessary more than once.

You cannot afford to miss their message.

Is anyone there?

This is the fundamental question. If God does not exist, searching for him is pointless. *For whoever would draw near to God must believe that he exists.*[1] While it is impossible to 'prove' God in a mathematical sense, the evidence is very convincing.

Take the existence of the universe. To call it the result of an 'accident' raises many questions — and answers none. The same is true of the 'Big Bang' theory. Where, for instance, did the raw materials come from? Not even a 'big bang' can make something out of nothing! The evolutionary idea is widespread, but just as weak; how can 'nothing' evolve into 'something', let alone earth's amazingly complex life forms?[2]

All other theories are equally fragile. The only satisfactory explanation is this: *In*

the beginning, God created the heavens and the earth. Our world is not the random result of a gigantic fluke involving ingredients that were 'always there'. Instead, *the universe was created by the word of God, so that what is seen was not made out of things that are visible.* Creation had a beginning, and it was God who brought it into being. *He spoke, and it came to be; he commanded, and it stood firm.*

This is reinforced by the amazing order and design seen everywhere and by the universal laws which hold everything together, from the vastness of outer space to microscopic organisms. But design demands a designer and laws a law-giver — and God is both! *The God who made the world and everything in it, being Lord of heaven and earth.*

But the strongest 'creation evidence' is man himself. Unlike other living creatures, man has something we call 'personality'; he makes intelligent choices, has a conscience and can distinguish between right and wrong. He is capable of love and compassion. Above all, he has an instinct to worship. Where did he get these qualities? Neither evolution nor an avalanche of accidents could have produced them. The clearest answer is this: *The LORD God formed the man of dust from the ground and breathed into his nostrils the breath of life, and the man became a living creature.* Man is not an accident; he is *fearfully and wonderfully made* by the Creator of the universe.

---

1. All words in italic type (other than book titles) are quotations from the Bible as indicated on page 55 onwards.

2. This is a major and complex issue, impossible to discuss here. If evolution is a genuine problem to you, read *From Nothing to Nature*, by Prof. E. H. Andrews (Evangelical Press).

Is God speaking?

The question is vital. Left to ourselves we are totally ignorant of God. *Can you find out the deep things of God? Can you find out the limit of the Almighty?* God is beyond our understanding and we need him to reveal himself to us.

Creation is one of the main ways in which he does so. *The heavens declare the glory of God, and the sky above proclaims his handiwork.* The sheer size of the universe and its amazing balance, variety and beauty reveal a great deal about the God who made it. In creation God shows his stupendous power, awesome intelligence and brilliant imagination. *For his invisible attributes, namely, his eternal power and divine nature, have been clearly perceived, ever since the creation of the world, in the things that have been made. So they are without excuse.*

When we communicate with one another we rely heavily on words. God also speaks to men through words — the words of the Bible. Nearly 4,000 times in the Old Testament alone (500 times in the first five books) you will find phrases like 'the Lord spoke', 'the Lord commanded', and 'the Lord said'. This is why it is claimed that *no prophecy was ever produced by the will of man, but men spoke from God as they were carried along by the Holy Spirit.*

In no other literature can we find scores of clear and detailed prophecies made by men claiming to speak from God, and later fulfilled to the letter. The odds against this happening by chance are too vast to be taken seriously.

Then there is the Bible's impact on people's lives. No other book has had such a life-changing power. Millions of people, over thousands of years, have proved by personal experience that *the law of the LORD is perfect, reviving the soul; the testimony of the LORD is sure, making wise the simple; the precepts of the LORD are right, rejoicing the heart; the commandment of the LORD is pure, enlightening the eyes*.

After 2,000 years no expert in any field has ever disproved a single statement in the Bible.[3] The reason is this: *All Scripture is breathed out by God.* We should therefore accept it *not as the word of men but as what it really is, the word of God.*

3. If you have serious questions about the Bible read *Nothing but the Truth*, by Brian Edwards (Evangelical Press).

What is God like?

This is obviously the next question to be faced. To acknowledge that God exists is one thing, and to acknowledge him in the general sense that God speaks to us in creation and through the pages of the Bible is another. But we need to know more. What is God actually like?

The Bible gives us many clear and positive answers to this tremendously important question. Here are some of them.

God is personal. God is not a 'thing', power or influence. He thinks, feels, desires and acts in ways that show him to be a living personal Being. But he is not just 'the man upstairs' or some kind of 'superman'. *The LORD is the true God; he is the living God and the everlasting King.*

God is one. There is only one true God. He says, *'I am the first and I am the last;*

besides me there is no god.' Yet God has revealed himself as a 'trinity' of three Persons — the Father, the Son (Jesus Christ) and the Holy Spirit, each of whom is truly, fully and equally God. The Bible speaks of *the glory of God the Father*; it says that *the Word* [Jesus Christ] *was God*; and it speaks of *the Lord who is the Spirit*. While there is only one God, there are three Persons in the Godhead.

God is spirit. He has no physical dimensions. He does not have a body, nor does he have any characteristics that can be defined in terms of size and shape. *God is spirit, and those who worship him must worship in spirit and truth.* This means that God is invisible. *No one has ever seen God.* It also means that he is not confined to one place at a time, but is everywhere all the time: *'Do I not fill heaven and earth? declares the* LORD.*'* Quite apart from anything else, this means that God is fully aware of everything that happens everywhere. This includes not only everything you do and say, but every thought that passes through your mind.

God is eternal. God has no beginning. In the Bible's words, *from everlasting to everlasting you are God*. There never was a time when God did not exist and there never will be a time when he will not exist. God describes himself as the one *who is and who was and who is to come*. And he remains eternally the same: *I the LORD do not change*. All that God ever was he still is and always will be.

God is independent. Every other living being is dependent on people or things,

and ultimately on God — but God is totally independent of his creation. He can survive on his own. *Nor is he served by human hands, as though he* needed anything, since he himself gives to all mankind life and breath and everything.

God is holy. *Majestic in holiness, awesome in glorious deeds.* There can be no comparison with the holiness of God. *There is none holy like the LORD*, who is utterly without fault or defect. The Bible says of him, *You who are of purer eyes than to see evil and cannot look at wrong.* And this holy God demands holiness from every one of us. His command to us today is: *You shall be holy, for I am holy.*

God is just. The Bible says that *the LORD is a God of justice* and that *righteousness and justice are the foundation of his throne.* God is not only our Creator and Sustainer; he is also our Judge, rewarding and punishing, in time and eternity, with a justice that is perfect and beyond any appeal or dispute.

God is perfect. His knowledge is perfect. *No creature is hidden from his sight, but* *all are naked and exposed to the eyes of him to whom we must give account.* God knows everything in the past, present and future, including all our thoughts, words and deeds. His wisdom is perfect and utterly beyond our understanding. *Oh, the depth of the riches and wisdom and knowledge of God! How unsearchable are his judgements and how inscrutable his ways!*

God is sovereign. He is the sole and supreme ruler of the universe, and nothing whatever is outside of his control. *Whatever the LORD pleases, he does, in heaven and on earth.* With God there are no accidents or surprises. He writes all the world's history and *works all things according to the counsel of his will.* God needs no advice or consent for anything he chooses to do. Nor can anyone prevent him doing what he pleases: *None can stay his hand or say to him: 'What have you done?'*

God is omnipotent. He is all-powerful. In his own words, *I am the LORD, the God of all flesh. Is anything too hard for me?* This does not mean that God can do anything (he cannot lie, or change, or make mistakes, or sin, or deny himself) but that he can do anything he wishes consistent with his character.

These are just brief sketches of some of the things God has revealed in the Bible about his own nature and character. There are other truths about God in the Bible (and we will look at one of these on page 38) though there are many things about him we cannot possibly understand. He *does great things and unsearchable, marvellous things without number.* In that sense, *the Almighty — we cannot find him* and no amount of human intelligence or reasoning can change that. This should hardly surprise us. If we could understand God he would be unworthy of our worship.

Who am I?

The pressures and problems of modern living are driving many people to a restless search for meaning and purpose in life. We have seen something of who God is; what about us? Why do we exist? Why are we here? Does human life have any meaning or purpose?

The first thing to get clear is that man does not merely 'exist'. He is more than an accidental accumulation of atoms which all happen to fit together into a convenient package we call 'a human being'. The Bible tells us that he was specifically created by a wise and holy God. *So God created man in his own image, in the image of God he created him; male and female he created them*. Man is more than a highly developed animal or refined ape. He is as different from other creatures as animals are from vegetables and vegetables are from minerals. In terms of size, man is

minute compared with the sun, moon and stars, but God has given him a unique and honoured place in the universe.

This is seen in one of God's first commands to man: *Have dominion over the fish of the sea and over the birds of the heavens and over every living thing that moves on the earth.* Man became God's personal representative on earth, with authority over all other living creatures. But man was also given special dignity. Being created 'in the image of God' does not mean that he was made the same size or shape as God (we have seen that God does not have 'size' or 'shape'), nor that man was a miniature of God, possessing all his qualities in small quantities. It means that man was created as a spiritual, rational, moral and immortal being, with a nature that was perfect. In other words he was a true reflection of God's holy character.

What is more, man gladly and constantly chose to obey all God's commands and as a result lived in perfect harmony with him. Man had no 'identity crisis' then! He knew exactly who he was and why he was in the world, and he obediently took his God-given place.

But not only was man totally fulfilled and completely satisfied with his position in the world, God was satisfied with man! We know this because the Bible tells us that when his work of creation was complete, with man as its crowning glory, *God saw everything that he had made, and behold, it was very good.* At that point in history, perfect people lived in a perfect environment in a perfect relationship with each other and in perfect harmony with God.

That is hardly the situation today! What happened?

What went wrong?

The straightforward answer to the question is this: *sin came into the world through one man, and death through sin.*

The first man and woman (Adam and Eve) were given great freedom, but also one serious warning: *But of the tree of the knowledge of good and evil you shall not eat, for in the day that you eat of it you shall surely die.* This was an ideal test of man's willingness to obey what God said simply because God said it. But the devil tempted Eve to disbelieve and disobey God's words, and she did. *When the woman saw that the tree was good for food, and that it was a delight to the eyes, and that the tree was to be desired to make one wise, she took of its fruit and ate, and she also gave some to her husband who was with her, and he ate.*

At that moment 'sin entered the world'.

By his deliberate disobedience man cut himself off from God. Instead of loving God, Adam and Eve were terrified of him: *the man and his wife hid themselves from the presence of the LORD God among the trees of the garden.* Instead of being assured, confident and happy, their sin had made them ashamed, guilty and afraid.

But God had said that man would die if he disobeyed, and he did. Death means separation, and in one terrible moment man became separated from God; he died spiritually. He also began to die physically, and now had a dead soul and a dying body. But that was not all: the children of Adam and Eve inherited their corrupt nature and sinful character. From then on, like pollution at the source of a river, the poison of sin has flowed to all Adam's descendants, and *so death spread to all men because all sinned.*

Notice that important word 'all', which obviously includes the writer and the reader of this page. We may never meet on this earth, but we have this in common — we are sinners and we are dying. *If we say we have no sin, we deceive ourselves, and the truth is not in us,* and if we claim not to be dying we are being ridiculous. Fooling around with the facts does nothing to change them.

Many of today's newspaper, television and radio headlines remind us of the fact that the world is in a mess. It is easy to condemn violence, injustice, disorder and wrongdoing in society, but before criticizing others ask yourself whether you are perfect and living a life pleasing to a holy God. Are you absolutely honest, pure, loving and selfless? God knows the answers to these questions — and so do you! *All have sinned and fall short of the glory of God.* You are a sinner by birth, by nature, by practice and by choice, and you urgently need to face the facts — and the consequences.

Is sin serious?

When disease is first diagnosed, it is important to ask the question: 'Is it serious?' It is even more important to ask that question about the spiritual disease of sin. Many people will almost cheerfully admit to being sinners, because they have no idea what this means. They treat it as being 'just human nature', or they shelter behind the fact that 'everybody does it'. But those statements dodge the real issue: is sin serious? Here are some of the things the Bible says about you as a sinner.

You are debased. This does not mean that you are as bad as you can possibly be, nor that you are constantly committing every sin. Nor does it mean that you cannot tell right from wrong, or do things that are pleasant and helpful. But it does mean that sin has invaded every part of your nature and personality — your mind, will, affections, conscience, disposition and

imagination. *The heart is deceitful above all things, and desperately sick.* The root of your trouble is not what you do but what you are! You sin because you are a sinner.

You are defiled. The Bible pulls no punches here: *For from within, out of the heart of man, come evil thoughts, sexual immorality, theft, murder, adultery, coveting, wickedness, deceit, sensuality, envy, slander, pride, foolishness.* Notice that the list includes thoughts, words and actions. This shows that in God's sight all sin is equally serious. Some people limit their idea of sin to things like murder, adultery and robbery, but the Bible makes it clear that we have no right to think of sin in this way. Sin is anything that fails to meet God's perfect standards. Anything we say, think or do that is less than perfect is sin. Now face up to this question: *Who can say, 'I have made my heart pure; I am clean from my sin'?* Can you? If not, you are defiled.

You are defiant. The Bible teaches that *sin is lawlessness*, deliberate rebellion against God's authority and law. No civil law forces you to lie, cheat, have impure thoughts, or sin in any other way. You choose to sin. You choose to break God's holy law. You deliberately disobey him and that is serious, because *God is a righteous judge, and a God who feels indignation every day.* God can never be 'soft' about sin, and you can be sure that not even one sin will go unpunished.

Some small part of God's punishment of sin comes in this life (though we may not recognize it). But the final punishment will be inflicted after death, when on the Day of Judgement *each of us will give an account of himself to God.*

Where do I go from here?

There are many ideas about what happens when we die. Some say we are all annihilated, some that we all go to heaven. Others believe in a place where sinful souls are prepared for heaven. But nothing in the Bible supports any of these ideas.

Instead, we read this: *it is appointed for man to die once, and after that comes judgement.* Those in a right relationship with God will then be welcomed into heaven, to spend eternity in his glorious presence. All others *will suffer the punishment of eternal destruction, away from the presence of the Lord and from the glory of his might.* The Bible's most common word for this is 'hell'. Here are four important truths about it:

Hell is factual. It is not something 'invented by the church'. The Bible says more about

hell than it does about heaven and leaves no doubt about its reality. It speaks of people being *sentenced to hell* and *thrown into hell.*

Hell is fearful. It is described in the Bible as a *place of torment; a fiery furnace;* a place of *everlasting burnings* and *unquenchable fire*. It is a place of suffering, with *weeping and gnashing of teeth* and in which there is *no rest, day or night.*

These are terrible words, but they are true. Those in hell are cut off from all good, cursed by God and banished from even the smallest help or comfort that his presence brings.

Hell is final. All the roads to hell are one-way streets. There is no exit. Between hell and heaven *a great chasm has been fixed*. The horror, loneliness and agony of hell are not in order to purify but to punish — for ever!

Hell is fair. The Bible tells us that God *will judge the world in righteousness* and he is perfectly just in sending sinners to hell. After all, he is giving them what they have chosen. They reject God here; he rejects them there. They choose to live ungodly lives; he confirms their choice — for ever. God can hardly be accused of injustice or unfairness!

In the light of these terrible truths, you need to think very carefully about a question once put to a group of people in the New Testament: *How are you to escape being sentenced to hell?*

Can religion help?

Man has been called a religious animal. *The Encyclopaedia of Religion and Ethics* lists hundreds of ways in which men have tried to satisfy their religious longings and feelings. They have worshipped the sun, moon and stars; earth, fire and water; idols of wood, stone and metal; fish, birds and animals. They have worshipped countless gods and spirits which have been the products of their own perverted imagination. Others have attempted to worship the true God through a vast variety of sacrifices, ceremonies, sacraments and services. But 'religion', however sincere, can never solve man's sin problem, for at least three reasons.

Religion can never satisfy God. Religion is man's attempt to make himself right with God, but any such attempt is futile because even man's best efforts are flawed and so are unacceptable to God. The Bible could not be clearer: *all our righteous deeds are like a polluted garment.* God demands perfection; religion fails to meet the demand.

Religion can never remove sin. Your virtues can never cancel out your vices. Good deeds can never remove bad ones. If a person gets right with God it is *not a result of works, so that no one may boast.* No religious efforts or experiences — christening, confirmation, baptism, holy communion, churchgoing, prayers, gifts, sacrifices of time and effort, Bible reading or anything else — can cancel out a single sin.

Religion can never change man's sinful nature. A person's behaviour is not the problem, only the symptom. The heart of man's problem is the problem of man's heart, and by nature man's heart is corrupt and depraved. Going to church and taking part in religious ceremonies may make you feel good, but they cannot make you good. *Who can bring a clean thing out of an unclean? There is not one.*

Some of the religious activities mentioned above are obviously 'good' in themselves. For example, it is right to go to church, to read the Bible and to pray, because God tells us to do these things. But you dare not rely on them to make you right with God. Not only are they powerless to do so; trusting in them actually adds to your sin and to your condemnation.

Is there an answer?

Yes there is! — and God has provided it. The central message of the Bible is summed up in these words: *For God so loved the world, that he gave his only Son, that whoever believes in him should not perish but have eternal life.*

We saw earlier that a just and holy God must punish sin. But the Bible also tells us that *God is love.* While God hates sin he loves sinners and longs to forgive them. But how can a sinner be justly pardoned when God's law demands his spiritual and physical death? Only God could solve that problem, and he did so in the person of Jesus Christ. *The Father has sent his Son to be the Saviour of the world.*

God the Son became a man by taking upon himself human nature. Although Jesus became fully man, he remained fully God: the Bible says that *in him the whole fulness of deity dwells bodily.* He remained as completely God as if he had not become man; he became as completely man as if he were not God. Jesus Christ is therefore unique and the Bible confirms this in many ways. His conception was unique; he had no human father but was conceived in a virgin's womb by the miraculous power of the Holy Spirit. His words were unique: people were *astonished at his teaching, for his word possessed authority.* His miracles were unique: he went about *healing every disease and every affliction among the people,* and on several occasions even raised the dead. His character was unique: he *was tempted as we are, yet without sin* so that God the Father could say of him, *'This is my beloved Son, with whom I am well pleased.'*

Notice that last sentence! This means that as a man Jesus kept the law of God in every part and therefore was not subject to sin's double death penalty. Yet he was arrested on a trumped-up charge, sentenced on false evidence, and eventually crucified at

Jerusalem. But his death was not a 'freak' or an unavoidable accident. It was all part of the *definite plan and foreknowledge of God.* The Father sent the Son for the very purpose of paying sin's death penalty, and Jesus willingly came. In his own words, the purpose of his coming into the world was *to give his life as a ransom for many.* His death, like his life, was unique.

This makes it vital that you understand what happened when Jesus died, and what his death can mean to you.

Why the cross?

All the Bible's teaching points to the death of Jesus. Neither his perfect life nor his marvellous teaching nor his powerful miracles are the focus of the Bible's message. These are all important, but above all else Jesus came into the world to die. What makes his death so important? The answer is that he died as a Substitute, a Sin-bearer and a Saviour.

Jesus the Substitute. This demonstrates the love of God. Sinners are guilty, lost and helpless in the face of God's holy law, which demands punishment for every sin. How can they possibly escape God's righteous wrath? The Bible's answer is this: *God shows his love for us in that while we were still sinners, Christ died for us.* As part of an amazing rescue plan God the Son volunteered to take the place of sinners and bear the just penalty for their sin. The sinless Son of God willingly suffered and died for them, *the righteous for the unrighteous.*

Jesus the Sin-bearer. This demonstrates the holiness of God. There was nothing 'faked' about Christ's death. The penalty for the sins of others was paid in full by the death of God's sinless Son. As he hung on the cross he cried out, *'My God, my God, why have you forsaken me?'* At that terrible moment God the Father turned his back on his beloved Son, who then endured the penalty of separation from God. Notice how this shows God's perfect holiness. All sin, every sin, must be punished — and when Jesus took the place of sinners he became as accountable for their sins as if he had been responsible for them. The one man who lived a perfect life suffered the double death penalty of the guilty.

Jesus the Saviour. This demonstrates the power of God. Three days after his death, Christ was *declared to be the Son of God in power according to the Spirit* *of holiness by his resurrection from the dead.* He *presented himself alive after his suffering by many proofs* and he will *never die again; death no longer has dominion over him.* In raising Christ from the dead, God powerfully demonstrated that he accepted his death in the place of sinners as the full and perfect payment of sin's penalty and as the basis on which he can offer a full and free pardon to those who would otherwise be doomed to spend eternity in hell.

But how does all this apply to you? How can you get right with God? How can Christ become your Saviour?

How can I be saved?

Having read this far, do you genuinely want to be saved? Do you want to get right with God — whatever the cost or consequences? If not, you have not grasped the importance of the pages you have read. You should therefore read them again, slowly and carefully, asking God to show you the truth.

If God has shown you your need, and you do want to be saved, then you must turn in *repentance towards God and have faith in our Lord Jesus Christ.*

You must repent. This means a complete change regarding sin. There must be a change of mind. You must admit that you are a sinner, a rebel against a holy and loving God. There must be a change of heart — genuine sorrow and shame at the vileness and filthiness of your sin. Then you must be willing to forsake it

and change the direction of your life. God challenges people to *perform deeds in keeping with their repentance.* You must do this. God will not forgive any sin you are not willing to forsake. To repent is to go in a new direction, seeking wholeheartedly to live in a way that pleases God.

You must have faith in Christ. First of all, this means accepting that Jesus is *the Christ, the Son of the living God* and that *Christ died for the ungodly.* Secondly, it means believing that in his power and love Christ is able and willing to save you. Thirdly, it means actually putting your trust in Christ, relying upon him and him alone to make you right with God. Your proud, sinful nature will fight against abandoning trust in your own 'goodness' or religion. Yet you have no alternative. You must stop trusting in anything else and trust only in Christ, who is *able to save to the uttermost those who draw near to God through him.*

If God has shown you your need, and given you this desire, then turn to Christ

— and do it now! Ideally, pray aloud to him; this may help you to be clear about what you are doing. Confess that you are a guilty, lost and helpless sinner, and with all your heart ask Christ to save you, and to take his rightful place as the Lord of your life, enabling you to turn from sin and to live for him.

The Bible says that *if you confess with your mouth that Jesus is Lord and believe in your heart that God raised him from the dead, you will be saved* and that *everyone who calls on the name of the Lord will be saved.* If you truly trust Christ as your Saviour and acknowledge him as your Lord, you can claim these promises as your own.

Which way now?

If you are now trusting in Christ there are many wonderful things in which you can rejoice. For instance, you are now in a right relationship with God: the Bible calls this being 'justified' and says that *since we have been justified by faith, we have peace with God through our Lord Jesus Christ.* Through Christ, your sins have been dealt with: *everyone who believes in him receives forgiveness of sins through his name.* You are now a member of God's family: all who trust in Christ are given *the right to become children of God.* You are eternally secure: *there is therefore now no condemnation for those who are in Christ Jesus.* God himself has come into your life in the person of the Holy Spirit: *the Spirit of him who raised Jesus from the dead dwells in you.* What great truths these are!

Now you need to grow in your new spiritual life. Here are four important things to which you will need to give close attention:

Prayer. You are now able to speak to God as your Father, something you have never been able to do before. You can worship him, praising him for his glory, power, holiness and love. You can ask for daily forgiveness. Not even those who become children of God are perfect, *but if we confess our sins, he is faithful and just to forgive us our sins and to cleanse us from all unrighteousness.* You can thank him every day for his goodness to you. There are so many things for which you will want to thank him, including the everyday benefits of life that we can so easily take for granted. But you will specially want to thank him for saving you, for accepting you into his family, and for giving you eternal life. You should never find it difficult to do this! You can also ask for his help, strength and guidance in your own life and in the lives of others. In particular, you will want to pray for other people you know who are away from God as you once were.

Bible reading. In prayer, you speak to God; in the Bible, God speaks to you. It is therefore very important that you read it every day, to *discern what is pleasing to the Lord.* As you do this, ask him to enable you to understand its meaning and to obey its teaching, so that *by it you may grow up to salvation.* If you need help in beginning to study the Bible, send for your free copy of the book mentioned on page 54.

Fellowship. Now that you have become a member of God's family, he wants you to meet regularly with your brothers and sisters! *Not neglecting to meet together ... but encouraging one another.* This means joining a local church, so make sure that you do this as soon as possible. Choosing the right church is not always easy, and you will want to find one which clearly believes and teaches the biblical truths you have been reading in these pages. The person who gave you this booklet should be able to help you. In your local church you will find out more about God; you will benefit from the experience of others;

you will learn the importance of God's special directions about baptism and holy communion; and you will discover the joy of sharing with others the gifts and abilities God has given you. You need the church, and the church needs you!

Service. It will now be your privilege to *serve the LORD your God with all your heart and with all your soul.* Always remember that God *has saved us and called us to a holy calling.* Make holiness an absolute priority. *For this is the will of God, your sanctification.* Then, seek to use your particular gifts in God's service; bear in mind that you *were created in Christ Jesus for good works.* Finally, be alert for opportunities of telling others *how much the Lord has done for you.* Telling others about Christ is not only the duty of those who trust him, it is an exhilarating experience!

From now on seek to live in such a way that in every part of your life *you may proclaim the excellencies of him who called you out of darkness into his marvellous light!*

If you have trusted Christ through reading this booklet, and would like help in your daily Bible reading, you are invited to write for a free copy of *Read, Mark, Learn,* a book of guidelines for personal Bible study based on Mark's Gospel. Please write to John Blanchard, c/o EP Books, Faverdale North, Darlington. DL3 0PH. England.

If you need further help, please contact the following person:

Bible references used in this book
are as follows:

Page 5
Hebrews 11:6
Genesis 1:1

Page 7
Hebrews 11:3
Psalm 33:9
Acts 17:24

Page 8
Genesis 2:7
Psalm 139:14

Page 9
Job 11:7
Psalm 19:1
Romans 1:20

Page 10
2 Peter 1:21

Page 11
Psalm 19:7-8
2 Timothy 3:16
1 Thessalonians 2:13

Page 12
Jeremiah 10:10
Isaiah 44:6

Page 13
Philippians 2:11
John 1:1
2 Corinthians 3:18
John 4:24
John 1:18
Jeremiah 23:24

Page 14
Psalm 90:2
Revelation 1:8
Malachi 3:6
Acts 17:25

Page 15
Exodus 15:11
1 Samuel 2:2
Habakkuk 1:13
1 Peter 1:16
Isaiah 30:18
Psalm 97:2

Hebrews 4:13

Romans 5:12

Page 16
Romans 11:33
Psalm 135:6
Ephesians 1:11
Daniel 4:35
Jeremiah 32:27

Page 25
1 John 1:8
Romans 3:23

Page 28
Jeremiah 17:9
Mark 7:21-22
Proverbs 20:9

Page 17
Job 5:9
Job 37:23

Page 29
1 John 3:4
Psalm 7:11
Romans 14:12

Page 18
Genesis 1:27

Page 20
Genesis 1:28

Page 30
Hebrews 9:27
2 Thessalonians 1:9

Page 21
Genesis 1:31

Page 32
Matthew 23:33
Matthew 5:29
Luke 16:28
Matthew 13:42
Isaiah 33:14
Matthew 3:12
Matthew 22:13
Revelation 14:11

Page 23
Romans 5:12
Genesis 2:17
Genesis 3:6

Page 24
Genesis 3:8

Romans 8:1
Romans 8:11

Page 49
1 John 1:9

Page 51
Ephesians 5:10
1 Peter 2:2

Hebrews 10:25

Page 52
Deuteronomy 10:12
2 Timothy 1:9
1 Thessalonians 4:3
Ephesians 2:10
Mark 5:19
1 Peter 2:9

Other resources you may find useful.

Why believe the Bible? by John Blanchard

How can we know that the present text in the Bible is anything like the original? Is it anything more than folklore? How can such an old book be relevant in the twenty-first century? Has science not taken its place as an explanation of the world and our place in it? Here are the answers.

Where do we go from here?
by John Blanchard

Where do we go from here? is the final question all humanity faces, and this booklet tackles it head-on.

Where is God when things go wrong?
by John Blanchard

Earthquakes, volcanoes, floods, hurricanes, fires, famine, and other natural disasters kill and injure millions of people, sometimes wiping out huge numbers within a few hours. Yet the Bible claims that God is in sole and sovereign control of everything that happens in the entire universe! How can that be?

Is anybody out there?
by John Blanchard

Ever since humankind has lived on earth we have been teased or tormented by questions that seem programmed into our humanity. 'Why am I here?'; 'Does life need to have any meaning?'; and the ultimate question: 'Is anybody out there?' This booklet explores the issues — and points to the answers.

Why on earth did Jesus come?
by John Blanchard

For many people, it is difficult to imagine Christmas without a whirlwind of giving and receiving presents. Yet millions who are delighted to accept gifts, large or small, refuse to accept the greatest gift ever offered — and one that can be theirs at any time of the year!

A wide range of Christian books is available from EP Books. If you would like a free catalogue please write to us or contact us by e-mail. Alternatively, you can view the whole catalogue online at our web site:

www.epbooks.org

EP BOOKS
Faverdale North, Darlington, DL3 0PH, England

e-mail: sales@epbooks.org

EP BOOKS USA
P. O. Box 614, Carlisle, PA 17013, USA

www.epbooks.us

e-mail: usasales@epbooks.org